FOUND IN TRANSLATION

A series of short plays and poems

This book is dedicated to those involved in the

project that sadly are no longer with us

FOUND IN TRANSLATION

A series of short plays and poems

Poems by care centre clients
Plays by Alexander Moschos and Hester Kent

The DOT Collective

Published under licence by Brown Dog Books and
The Self-Publishing Partnership, 7 Green Park Station, Bath BA1 1JB

www.selfpublishingpartnership.co.uk

ISBN: 978-1-78545-206-2

Cover design by Kevin Rylands
Internal design by Andrew Easton

Printed and bound by CPI Group (UK) Ltd, Croydon CR0 4YY

CONTENTS

INTRODUCTION

I'll start by mentioning who inspired me to set up The Dot Collective charity and how *Found In Translation* came to light. I grew up as a child actress, and my Nan, Dorothy (also known as Dot) quite often chaperoned me on film sets and in the theatre.

About two years ago my Nan was in need of constant care and moved into a care home in East Sussex. It was a brilliant care home, with a wide variety of activities. However, there wasn't anything available such as an event like theatre, at least not often enough or to a professional standard.

One day when I went to visit my Nan, she wasn't very happy and only wanted to stay in her room, despite a list sitting on the bedside table of activities such as carpet bowls, cookery and quiz sessions available to her.

When trying to encourage her to get out of her room and be involved socially she said: 'I can't do those things, my hands don't work anymore, I think I'll just go back to sleep.'

Then she asked me what I was up to and I told her I was acting in a show in London.

She replied: 'I wish I could see you do that, I wish I could do just any of the things I used to be able to do.' It was this conversation that gave me an idea.

I asked my Nan: 'What if I brought theatre here, to you? What would you like to *see?*'

She said: 'Oh yes, a bit of everything, please.'

Seeing the lucid smile on her face, gave me an equal sense of joy. I said: 'Done, let's do it.'

So then we got started, and planned our first tour for that Christmas. Unfortunately my Nan passed away just a week before we made it to her care home with the show. However, from the expression on her face at the thought of this idea and, after a brilliant Christmas, meeting generations of families sat together in the care home environment, I knew in that instant that this work was of great importance, for anyone who is unable to get out to do the things they once enjoyed. I quickly learnt that theatre of this form is beneficial to both those receiving care; working in care and for the arts, so we had to make it continue because theatre offers stimulation as well as shared entertainment without the pressure of having to participate in something that anxiety and immobility can stop you from doing. And this is when I decided to register The Dot Collective as a charity.

In the last two years we have toured professional productions of classic plays to care homes as full-scale productions that pop up in the living/dining rooms and gardens of care centres. With a professional team, we transform their spaces in front of their eyes bringing the aesthetics that one would expect when going to the theatre.

It was in response to the residents we met during these performances that inspired the idea of creating new work in care. After a show, so many of our audience members would tell us their stories and how they'd once donned the stage; written poetry, books, enjoyed the local dance hall and played music. They were often quite vocal throughout the show as well, eager to be involved. As a producer, one of the difficulties of providing this entertainment was finding the balance between providing a story that's stimulating by being something they can relate to while maintaining the level of professional, innovative and contemporary theatre that we set out to achieve. Therefore, we thought we'd try to created plays based on their thoughts, emotions, aspirations and memories. Which is when *Found In Translation* came into play.

The title of this project is based on the fact that dementia can create a barrier in communication, and often causes frustration between the person living with the disease and the carer/loved one. So rather than this difficulty to understand these thoughts and memories being a barrier and 'lost in translation' we wanted to use the language, movement, sound and shared moments to create new writing, finding something positive, beautiful and fresh from the collaboration between our team and the clients.

Found In Translation is a theatre project that actively involved and engaged those living with dementia and memory problems in care centres in the UK. The project was split into three key parts.

I. CREATIVE WRITING WORKSHOPS IN CARE

A company made up of professional actors, playwrights and a director conducted a number of one-hour storytelling workshops, where the residents and service users were encouraged to share their ideas, favourite music, write poetry, short stories and enjoy a theatrical environment.

In the first of these workshops our team created short stories with the clients by asking them to find a place from a photograph, a character from an item of clothing for the purpose of creating an improvised, fictional conversation between them. In our second series of workshops we focused on creative writing techniques by asking each person "what have you always wanted to be?" This question allowed the individual to be imaginative and inventive if they wanted to but more often than not, these characters became the person that they are. Stories were created from remembering their past and their most vivid memories. The workshops were a fascinating, touching, highly entertaining and valuable experience for The Dot Collective.

You will see in the first section of this book, some of the responses to the workshops and the many stories that were gold dust for our playwrights to develop.

2. PROFESSIONAL POP-UP THEATRE FOR CARE CENTRES

Playwrights Alexander Moschos and Hester Kent then developed the clients' ideas into a series of short plays, which were rehearsed to performance standard. These plays were then performed by professional actors back to the clients who took part in the workshops in the form of our pop-up theatre including a full lighting rig, sound, live music and all the sensory elements one would expect when going to the theatre. Alongside this, we held public performances during dementia awareness week to raise a positive awareness of the disease.

3. THE BOOK

The final stage is this book. We want to celebrate the abilities of the people we met, who were key collaborators in creating the plays. We have collated all the poems, short stories and finished plays into a book and each individual involved in the project will receive a copy that they can share with their friends and family and hopefully feel a sense of achievement.

There are 850,000 people in the UK with a diagnosis of dementia and 70% of people living in care homes have dementia or severe memory problems. We met so many bold characters, with fascinating pasts, ideas and senses of humour. Their thoughts and memories, noted down through poetical form has been a joy to read again when putting this book together and all of this has given such colour to these plays. I hope you enjoy reading them as much as I do.

Laura Harling – Artistic Director of The Dot Collective

POEMS & SHORT STORIES

POEMS BY THOSE AT WAYFIELD AVENUE, BRIGHTON AND HOVE

Eric the Idiot
I used to swim around the pier
The West pier it was
I was a good swimmer
I never got into any trouble
The lifeguard told me not to
But I was free
"What do you know about me getting into trouble?"
I'm safe.
I married him I did.
And I still went swimming round that pier
And I loved it, I did.

By Jeannette, Carol & Dorothy

Hot Place in India
Once upon a time in India
An eccentric old man became a hero
On a windy ol' day
And the silly buggers
Went on their way.

By Iris, Heather & Ron

Yellowy Sand

They were on a fun holiday
Dressed casually
There was yellowy sand
They were rowing about not being dressed right!

Anon

A Rocket

Get me on that rocket
I need a break
I need a rest from my kids
Cos I've got seven!

I've had enough of cooking and washing
I want an easy life
But I will remember to pack my husband
So I can love him while I can
And we can come back with seven more!

Anon

Healthy 90-year-old

I don't know
I'm 90-years-old!
Once I've spoken I've forgotten.
I've got a good family that look after me
I've always got them at the end of the phone
So what I forget
They remember.
What have I got to think about now?
I think I'd rather fly than go on a boat.

By Iris

Difference

My grandmother always said
"You get back what you put in."
And I think that's very true.
One thing I do remember
There were no sell-by dates on the foods in supermarkets.
That's what makes the world go round
The difference.

By Iris

The Moon

I'm going to the moon.
Why?
Because it's there.
I would like it
I like to be nosy and know what's there.
I've been looking up at it for a long time.
No-one's alive up there
Not as far as I know anyway.

By Joyce

Peter Pan

Peter Pan we're going into space!
Oh.
I'm not going.
Why? Why wouldn't you want to come?
Because. I'm not interested.
I'm going in the car to France.

Anon

Up, Up and Away

The rocket's fuelled and off we go
We're going to the moon you know.
It's just up there so I'm told
I wish that I were feeling bold.
We've packed our stuff
It's quite a lot
There isn't much we haven't got.
The mums are here, the children too
The nursing staff were number two.
We're going to float around a bit
But Nick is here to keep us fit.
Esther is Peter Pan,
But I don't know why coz she's not a man!

By Kitty

Flight Attendant

Throw them on the plane
Tell them what to do
Be a bit bossy
Cheeky and tricksy.
Will not serve tea or cake
Will not jump out the plane
Not even with a parachute. No!
Throw them off.

By Dorothy

POEMS AND SHORT STORIES BY THOSE AT THE PHOENIX CENTRE, LEWES

18th century Alan Sugar

This is a story of 18th century Alan Sugar. Almost anywhere, on an island near a castle in Dover, there was a 18th century businessman, a crow that wants to be pretty, a postman on a train who checks his watch every 10 minutes and a rogue fishmonger.

The crow who wants to be pretty (also known as Birdman) lives on the island guarding a shipwreck that lies underneath. This shipwreck offers the possibility of gold from a treasure chest. However, Birdman wants to set up a sanctuary but won't set up a bird sanctuary until he knows what to do with all the seagulls and puffins.

The banker comes to the island to build a hotel to make money because profit is what he likes. He is dubious of the rogue fishmonger and starts taxing him on any fish he catches from his seas.

The man on the train is going on holiday to the island, wearing his expensive waistcoat, as he will have lots of tea and dinner with the fishmonger. Little do they all know of the property tycoon who will offer an age of enlightenment!

By D.R. & Ian Brechin

The Teacher
They're willing to learn
To do their best to earn
They write to show their way
And sometimes, to play.

By Betty Hampton

Success
You need drive
And a plan
And then find somebody else to do the work
And that's how one is successful

By Gregory Smith

Driver
I'm driving my limousine
Where am I going?
It all depends.
I used to drive on the 07 to New Haven
When one of these beautiful drivers went into me
I went off the road
Into a waterhole.
It was a lovely car.
It's back on the road,
I see it every now and then.
I'd love to have it back
I'd just take off.
It was so, so beautiful.

By John Tiller

Farmer

I used to be a farmer
I used to milk the cows and feed the calves.
And we had a bull.
If the cow wants servicing, you'd have to get the bull out.
I had 65 animals and I gave them all names.
Milk in the morning
Milk at night.
Take the milk home.

By Donald John Groves

Pro Cyclist

Rolling hillsides
Hot tarmac
Tired legs
Stopping at pubs (gotta get that one in somewhere)
Being good with friends
Sharing ups and downs

By Mr Ted

First-Class Idiot
I basically buy sweets to give away
They used to call me the sweetie man until I packed up
And came this way
I don't buy many these days
I give one away here and there
It's amazing what I gained giving the sweets away
People would help me out
And it worked out cheap
If you know what I'm saying!

By Bob White

My name
A Cooper is a barrel maker
It's a dying trade the barrels now
They're mainly made of metal
Harvey's now use metal.
I was with them 15 years
A cooper is a barrel maker
They're mainly made of metal now.

By John Arthur Cooper

POEMS BY THOSE AT CLAYDON HOUSE, LEWES

A Prayer

Here all of us are
We must observe the goodness of all
And show no rudeness. We are all together.
As one team
We must observe the goodness
Of that
Kindness is a quality we must never forget.

By Louis

The Hippy Story

I'm going along with you
She's been and buggered that up now.
You look nice, very pretty
Hash cake?
It's a lovely day, let's enjoy ourselves.
It's nice here
There's a great festival down the road
Everyone's going there.
Do you want to go?
They say the Beatles might be here.
I'd love to go.
It would be great if we could dance with the Beatles!

By Jenny & Gladys

We Can All Enjoy Eating

Audrey goes out hunting and returns with a pheasant
Welcomed by Louis the gatekeeper
Who is listening to Mozart
And drinking
Waiting for the bird to be ready to eat.
Off to bed
Dreaming of a pilgrimage to a temple with Borneo the dog.
Louis waves goodbye to his gate
Joining Audrey on her pilgrimage to the red and gold temple.

By Audrey & Louis

A Boater And A Rambler

A wedding on a sunny terrace
A father of the bride
Biodegradable confetti
And a photo of us waving goodbye.
The first dance
A father and his daughter
Sea, clouds, fish and chips
Sounds of seagulls, Guinness.
Waiting…
We waited for our captain
Who didn't turn up
So the beefeater drove the boat.

By Patricia & Betty

Robin

A robin sings,
Outside my window.
He flys down to the ground
But never stays around.
He doesn't really sing at all,
Just taps along
He's a lovely little fellow.
One day he brought his girlfriend,
Or wife.
But they didn't stay long
They sang
They picked a little bread
Do you know how much a robin eats?
Not much.
But the squirrels came
And they flew away.
So they didn't stay long.
I haven't seen them for a while
Actually.

By Audrey

In their Nature
The cat will run after the poor creature
It's in their nature.
I'll clap my hands rather hard
To frighten him off
But we mustn't forget
It is in their nature.
That's what the good lord said, anyway.

By Rita

Lord of the Manor
Poetry brings a different world to you
It brings things as I would like them to be
And not as they are.
How would I like things to be?
That is a big question
Too big to answer in such a short time.
To be Lord of the manor
In a big house
I'd feel neutral.
I don't want to be in a big house
But I don't want not to be in a big house.
If I was to write a poem
The first thing that comes to mind
Is to write a woman's beauty
I would also like to write about scenery and environment.

By Lawrence

The Church Bell

The only bell in the tower
Start to ring at 8am
To get people up,
Get them to church.
I can see beautiful gardens in the village
Well looked after
Nursery house full of families
I'm a golden bell,
Medium sized
Loud,
Pleasant sounding bell.

By Joan

POEMS AND SHORT STORIES BY THOSE AT KNOLL HOUSE, BRIGHTON & HOVE

A Peaceful Place
Together we celebrate
How he came looking for money
And went away eating toast.
Suits her to a T.

Anon

ATS
You go up and up
That's if you're well in,
Learn to keep your beds made
And all things like that.
Nowadays, they give the special jobs to do.
You just get told what to do.
You could be shoved in the canteen
Or you could be shoved somewhere else.
You could be anywhere.
The most modern barracks is Aldershot
Even when I worked in the British shops
I was opposite the barracks.

Anon

Straps On The Past

I like women, a womaniser you might say.
If you saw her now you'd be struck dumb
Even in her later years
She is so beautiful
Outstandingly so.
I like Ingrid Bergman for a start
And I'll classify her as outstanding too
But is Ingrid more so than she?
That, well, I can't say.
It's all straps on the past.

Anon

Dry Cleaning

When I was 19, I was called up by the government to join the army
and if you were lucky enough you could chose where to go. So
I wanted to join the RAF, and I did! After the war I went back to
work at Flynn's – the dry cleaners, and I was pregnant, so I was
happy. My husband and I met six weeks before I was posted, in St
Mary's dance hall.

Anon

Out of Two

I've got two children
But I ended up with sixteen grandchildren
Seven on my son's side
And nine on my daughter's side
In America.
Out of two!
I only had two children
Christmas is difficult
I used to buy for them all but it got too much
I'm 94.

Anon

A Book Illustrator

Draw a picture of a land mind landscape
In a picture of trees and fields and trees,
Houses and houses,
Horses, fields, trees…

Anon

POEMS BY THOSE AT CRAVEN VALE, BRIGHTON & HOVE

Lavender Fields
On a barren field in France
Where the lavender flowers dance
The yellow sun shone overhead
And it got too hot for Fred.

Anon

Fred's Holiday in Spain
His holiday in Spain was due
He couldn't wait to see the view
As he stood on the grassy mountains
Watching the Alhambra fountains.

Anon

Gertie's Golden Eggs
Eating toast is the most boring occupation in the world
And my mother was wrong
My hair never curled
Through eating my crusts
– A saying that everyone trusts.

Anon

Cleaning
Once upon a time there was a carriage cleaner called Joan.
She had to balance on things to clean the ceiling
And she listened to music on the radio.
Heaven knows how I managed to keep my balance
But I did.
And that's the story of Joan the cleaner.

Anon

The Dance Hall
When I went dancing
I'd wear a nice dress with a full skirt
It looks nice when you're doing the quick step.
But that wasn't important
You had to remember the right steps to the dance
You'd soon enough see if someone's not a dancer
They have two left feet!

Anon

POEMS BY THOSE AT NORTON HOUSE, WESTMINSTER

Seychelles

I can't lounge in hammocks
Because I'll end up sinking
Nature provides the commedia dell arte
I wouldn't like to hang about there long.
A stanza with its all obliterated tongue
Murmured gently
Brother gently prays.

By Peter

A Poet And A Singer

Once when we went to the Caspian Sea to swim
In that special place meant for the army –
Still on the Iranian side, not the Russian…
Amongst the mountains and the rivers.

By Azizeh

Florist
One morning,
They wanted to take it
I was upstairs
And I thought who was that up there?
I went to Covent Garden market
It was a hell of a road
And they were all working
I started looking and asking and I said
'I can't believe it'
They were taking all the flowers,
From another shop
They had those great big what's your names.
I said
I've never told you to take those!

Anon

Something Nice
My grandmother
I grew accustomed to her
I wish I could have seen my mother more
Everyone a little more.
But that's life

By Millicent

Hi

Your colleague lacks underwear – deliberate?
Or accidental?
Yellow socks deeply rolled.

By Hilary

I Am

I am a very happy and sociable character
I enjoy all the activities at Norton House
I have strong faith in my God
Although we do not have regular Mass.
I do not take risks
Because my arm is broken sweetie.

Anon

I Wanted To Be

I always wanted to be walking
I never liked sitting down too long.
I always wanted to be mixing with people
I never liked boring work.
That's why the doctors say
'You are strong'.

By Millicent

Doctor Maria

I was a secretary
My aim was to be a doctor.
When I was working as a secretary
They appointed me as a doctor.
I used to take her to the hospital
Her name was Maria.

By Piera

Tennis

You hit the ball
And you carry on
Until the next one
Drops.

By Sheila

Dancer

Big energies, not very little
It is also a country
You know there is a country
And the place?
The people are very sad
They talk to you
And remember that they want to write on paper.

By Maria G

The Escape

Amar was trying to catch a burglar
The burglar flew to Italy
And escaped.

By Deborah

Lady of Leisure

The lady of leisure is on a campsite
They were partying and eating fish
Which was nice.
She has six hundred friends
But not all of them were there.

Anon

The Dancer

The dancer was on the island
But he couldn't dance, No!
He wants to be free, Si!

By Fernando

Cricket Player

He could sign autographs
He could be good with nature
Plays as the team's captain in hot climates
India, Pakistan, Australia and all of it.
He could get on a boat to take him down the river.

Anon

Dancing

Dancing
Dancing
Dancer in the heat
Dancing

By Fernando

Sister Benedict

When I came over,
I was a sad little girl
Staying with a Jewish family.
Then I came to London –
Trained as a nurse in Hyde Park corner.
I have 3 degrees from LSE
Sociology
A Masters and a PhD.
I worked as a ward sister for the Department of Health
And then imperial college for several years of wealth.
Then it came upon me,
A bad period of depression
I retired at 60
And started my recession.
I lost faith,
A serious depression.
Margaret looked after me
I couldn't live without my faith.
Dear Lord,
Thank you for keeping Maria safe
And if I die before I wake
I ask you Lord
To offer my soul to you.

Anon

POEMS BY THOSE FROM ETAT AT THE THAMESBANK CENTRE, WESTMINSTER

Going into Space
Up, up and away
To the infinite heavens
Landing in one planet to another
Dreading the meteors coming my way.
Hoping to return back to planet Earth.

By Lorma

Trampolines
Jumping up and down and landing
On my bottom.
Seeing lots of things I should not.
But I would be enjoying myself
Seeing how other people live.
Love and laughter makes the world a happy place
I hope with all my friends around.

By Dorothy Styles

Pirate

A tall, thin, blond pirate
Feeds his parrot
Finds some treasure
Creates a map.
Dances to a hornpipe
Sings sea shanties
Drinks run (err!)
Sweeps the decks and flys the Jolly Roger
Sailing the Seven Seas.
Retire rich and famous.

Anon

A writer and poet

I look at the sky
And it's changing hue
To give inspiration
To the writing I do.
I look all around
To get inspiration
So I don't write in desperation.
I visit the library and places of interest
Do interviews and wear elegant clothes.
Sit down and write of the past remembered
And places I've seen far and near.
I illustrate what I've written about
And read stories aloud.

By Margaret Hiscock

The Rainbow Café Owner

I've had a dream for many years
But my head is in the trees
I'll never forget my perfect dream
And hope one day it's as it seems.

By Ann

The Reporter

There was a reporter who tried
When he lost his job he cried
Oh poor me
I wanted to be
The best I could.

By Constance Bizzell

The Dancer

In my dreams I dance around
With music and happiness all around.
One day this will happen
And I shall be a very happy lady.

By Ruby

Orator

Important place with important people
I hope I could say something steering
That would have them all listening to me
And give me wonderful applause
I would feel really, really high and wonderful.
Then I'd find somewhere nice and tranquil.

By Kathleen

The Writer

I am a writer and I love to drink
When the book is finished.
When I don't have to think
anymore
I love to write books and research on a computer
Because the computer does spell checks.

Anon

POEMS AND SHORT BY THOSE AT IRELAND LODGE, BRIGHTON & HOVE

Captain

I was born in Norway
And off I went to sea one sunny day.
I have travelled the world as a merchant seaman
To Saudi Arabia
Kicked out of Canada
Witnessed a murder on board the ship
And in a bar
But oh what an exciting life have I had.

Anon

Knitted House

I bought a pattern from Bellman's
To knit my house of wool.
My house will be white
My house has four windows with blue curtains,
A knitted vase of pink flowers is in my garden.
One morning at 6am
When I was just getting up to have my knitted cup of tea,
The howling winds blew my knitted house away.
Unbelievably, my knitted pink flowers remained in my garden
And never blew away!
I remained safe and made another house of white.
Click, click, click!

Anon

Knitted House 2

If you get the wool
For me,
A pair of needles too,
I will knit a house
For you,
And a pair of baby shoes.

Anon

Caravan Life

In a mobile caravan somewhere in Ireland, Gerry was in his burger
van, when a fight broke out. So he had a few words with these
people, they were a bit uptight and breathing heavily. The fight
broke out because the burger van had run out of burgers. This
burger van got so busy, Gerry had to shut up for two hours to
restock; which the two fighters didn't like at all. Two police cars
pulled up that Gerry knew and he passed over the responsibility.
This all created a good atmosphere around his van; the police
couldn't get out their doors quick enough on a Monday morning to
come for a burger!

Anon

A wealthy woman and the millionaire

We've just bought Buckingham Palace off the Queen because she's a bit hard up. We paid loads of money for it. Well I did, wealthy woman here didn't have much so I had to help her out. We moved in and had a walk about to see how much work needed doing. Not much at all it turns out, the servants can do all that anyway. So, we're heading out to the garden with the animals. It's a beautiful garden; there are gardeners in it and loads of dogs. Massive. How would you walk around that place we thought? Lot of men on it. Some are good. Actually, they're all good and safe but we wouldn't have a cup of tea with them, we're royalty. We'd run out of teabags! We've put Prince Charles on a lead so we know where he is. We go out on the horses because that's what we do. Then, one day, we put some money on the races and had a big win. They say you can never have too much money. Money makes money. It makes the world go round. We decided to give some of it to the poor and then we're going to have a good time. Go out. Have a drink! Have a dance. See some shows. Do everything that we couldn't do before. Then we're going to have a party. But first, we'll check on the Queen. See if she's all right. Give her a shandy. We don't want to give her whisky, that's too expensive. She can't afford it.

Anon

Farmer Giles

We're on a farm in West Sussex, which is owned by farmer Giles. It's situated amongst the beautiful countryside for everyone to take it all in. He is taking care of his cattle and checking the ewes are okay. He notices a broken fence and one or two animals have got through (it happens quite often). The farmer calls for his sheep dogs to round up the cattle that have escaped and they are brought back safely. He fixes the fence with his helpers, quietly repairs it with more timber and wooden posts. He is pleased that none of the animals are injured and thanks his staff and dogs for doing a good job.

Anon

Land Lady of The Bat and Ball

She'd be behind the bar
For people to drink Alcohol!
No food
But Crisps.
My husband and me go to that pub.
She wears natural clothes that always look nice on
She doesn't interfere with anything,
Just does her service.

Anon

PLAYS

Francis, Oh Francis!, *Under Wood Island*, *The Dead Zone* and *Love's Hero* were first performed on tour during dementia awareness week 2017 (15^{tth}-21st May) to nine care centres in Lewes, Brighton and London and at The Blue Elephant Theatre, Southwark and The Friends Meeting House, Brighton with the following company:

ACTORS	Hester Kent
	Chris Levens
	Alys Scratchley
	Stuart Turner
WRITERS	Alexander Moschos, Hester Kent
DIRECTOR	Maja Milatovic-Ovadia
STAGE MANAGER	Ariel Harrison
PRODUCER & DESIGNER	Laura Harling
MUSIC	Allan Clayton

FRANCIS, OH FRANCIS!

(Or, The Mystery of The Trouser Less Man and The Missing Vase)

BY ALEXANDER MOSCHOS

This was inspired by three characters created by service users at Knoll House in Brighton & Hove, which centred on a retired trouserless butler by the name of Francis. Francis has a natural inclination to steal things and cared little about the other characters he found himself meeting on a beautiful island in the Caribbean ocean – his priority; money and a missing Ming vase.

Characters
Francis
Jimmy / Douglas
Sister Janet / Theresa

Lavish room in what might be a very grand hotel, or maybe it's the master bedroom in a big mansion. Either way it's very big and luxurious – if a little dusty.

On an armchair in the middle of the room an older gentleman (but with a surprisingly youthful face) in what looks like the attire of a butler is sitting with his legs carefully covered in a nice blanket and resting on a footstool.

By the door stands a young man, by what he's wearing we can assume that he is a bellboy.

The room is silent, though it is very apparent that the man in the armchair wants to talk but for some reason despite that want, a discourse feels very far away.

After what feels like a very long and slightly awkward time, the young man gives in.

Jimmy	Sir?
Francis	Yes, Jimmy?
Jimmy	Was there something you wanted, sir?
Francis	No, I don't think so

Pause

Jimmy	Very well. Sir

Pause

The older man starts to look around the room uncomfortably

After a while:

Francis	Oh I do wish you'd ask me again!
Jimmy	What sir? *(Beat)* Oh, Is there something you wanted, sir?
Francis	Oh Jimmy, you don't have to call me sir
Jimmy	Yes, sir
Francis	We're both servants after all
Jimmy	Indeed, sir
Francis	There you go on doing it again
Jimmy	But, sir
Francis	Jimmy!
Jimmy	Yes, but, sir
Francis	Now you're really being impossible and quite frankly a little rude
Francis	I don't know your name...sir

Pause

Francis	Oh, have I not told you?
Jimmy	No, sir
Francis	I can't say that surprises me!
Jimmy	Why is that?

Francis	Well, it's Francis
Jimmy	Oh.
Francis	Yes and before you say anything, don't bother, I know exactly what you're thinking
Jimmy	And what would that be...Francis?
Francis	How a man like me could have a name such as Francis
Jimmy	Well?
Francis	Yes I too have always thought it strange, yes it's queer...
Jimmy	I'm not sure I follow
Francis	Francis. It seems to me a name more suited to a man of some standing, a man with morals, maybe even a little...delicate. Such a name does not suit a lousy person like myself.
Jimmy	Why not change it?
Francis	The thought has struck me, but a name is very much like a shadow. Sure depending on the time of day or where you stand, you can rid yourself of it. But only momentarily. It always comes back! It'll follow you around, however much you wish it didn't.
Jimmy	I think it suits you. Although...
Francis	Although?

Jimmy   Well I always thought of it as a woman's name.

Francis   Now you're being positively cruel

Jimmy   I'm sorry, sir

Francis   No, no…I deserve it. A moral failure like myself

Jimmy   I wish you'd refrain from speaking about yourself in that manner! What could you possibly have done to think of yourself so harshly?

Francis   Oh Jimmy, I wouldn't even know where to start.

Jimmy   Why don't you try at the beginning?

Francis   It's not that simple…bad habits are somewhat…circular…after a while it's hard to know where one wicked plan started and where the next horrible decision ended. And so, it goes round and round in a big wheel of nastiness. I never seemed to make it stop. One cruelty after another. It is shameful but once the wheel started spinning…it just seemed to gather speed. It's hard to keep up with my bad deeds.

Jimmy   Put a stick in it?

Francis   A stick?

Jimmy   Yes, put a stick in the wheel. It'll jam it and make it stop spinning.

Francis	I wish you wouldn't humour me like that. It's patronising.
Jimmy	I do not mean to patronise you, Francis. I'm merely trying to find out what you've done to think so badly of yourself.
Francis	Oh my dear Jimmy, if I told you, it would mean I'd make you an accomplice and I couldn't do that to you. Your soul is pure.
Jimmy	It might ease your mind not to carry the burden of whatever it is on your own.

Pause

Jimmy	Well then, go on, what is it that weighs so heavy on your heart?
Francis	There have been so many dirty dealings and broken promises, but...
Jimmy	But?
Francis	But there's one thing in particular. Something that was in my possession. Something very valuable.
Jimmy	But is not in your possession anymore?
Francis	Well, it is and it isn't
Jimmy	I don't understand. How can it be both?
Francis	See, what if I told you...

They're interrupted by the loud chime of a doorbell.

Jimmy doesn't move seemingly still expecting Francis to finish his sentence.

Francis   Shouldn't you attend to that?

Jimmy   Yes, sir.

Jimmy heads towards the door.

Francis   And don't let anyone in before telling me who it is!

Jimmy   Yes, sir

Francis   And don't let them know whether I am here or not before consulting me!

Jimmy   Yes, sir

Jimmy leaves

Once Francis is alone in the room he stands up on the armchair throwing the blanket that's been carefully wrapped around his legs across the room. He is not wearing any trousers.

He starts to do a bit of a dance. There's something almost childlike about his movements. A young nun enters the room. Francis does not notice and continues dancing.

Sister Janet   Where are your trousers, child?

Francis   Huh!

Sister Janet: Francis! Where are your trousers?

Francis: I don't know.

Sister Janet	Now what have we said about lying Francis?
Francis	I'm not lying!
Sister Janet	So? Where are your trousers?
Francis	I DON'T KNOW!
Sister Janet	And to lie about telling a lie does not make it truth! On the contrary it makes it worse. Do not entangle yourself in lies, young man. It is a web very hard to free yourself from.
Francis	Maybe I never had any trousers. Have you ever thought of that?
Sister Janet	Don't be foolish, Francis!
Francis	Argh! I'm bored!
Sister Janet	That might be so but even bored young boys need to wear trousers! And you're not bored, you're just lazy. There is no such thing as boredom in this world. Only lack of ambition.
Francis	I don't fancy wearing trousers today!
Sister Janet	Francis, one should not give in to fancies. No wonder you say you're bored. To fancy is an unspecific want. In other words you want nothing and when you want nothing, nothing is what you get in return – you'll end up stuck in an abyss of nothingness!
Francis	Well, I still don't want to wear any trousers.

FOUND IN TRANSLATION

Sister Janet   Francis!

Francis   You can't make me!

Sister Janet   Oh I sure can!

Francis   You just try!

Sister Janet   You /

Francis   If you can catch me!

Francis jumps off the chair and starts running around the room, Sister Janet runs after him. What ensues is a rather violent yet affectionate game of tag. Finally in a fit of laughter from them both Sister Janet catches Francis.

Francis   *(through laughter)* I'm not wearing trousers today

Sister Janet   You - Well then I'm just going to have to/

She goes to smack him on the bottom but stops herself and instead starts to tickle him - this is something that he obviously enjoys

Once they've caught their breaths after all the laughing

Janet   You see Francis the world is such a wonderful place and there is so much beauty in it. Beauty is in everything, you just have to want to see it. When you decide to see the beauty you'll never want to unsee it. And when you choose to take part in all the wonders of the world you'll never be bored again...

Pause

Francis	Sister Janet?
Janet	Yes, Francis

Pause

Francis	Does anyone love me?

Beat

Sister Janet	Of course
Francis	Who?
Sister Janet	God. God loves you. God loves everyone
Francis	Who else?

Beat

Sister Janet	I do, Francis. I love you

She embraces him. As she does so Francis smacks her on the bottom and runs off

Francis	Still not wearing any trousers though!

She gets up and leaves

Francis	Stupid trousers. Stupid Sister Janet.

He stands up on the armchair again. Suddenly there's a loud thump.

A man has entered the room. He is blind and is struggling to find his way. Bumping into things.

Francis	When did I hire you?...Did I hire you?
Jimmy	Yes, you did, sir.
Francis	Oh. What are your working hours?
Jimmy	I'm here all the time, sir?
Francis	All the time?
Jimmy	At your service.
Francis	Do I pay you? Please tell me I pay you!
Jimmy	You do, sir.
Francis	And you really ought to have the weekends off.
Jimmy	Thank you, sir.
Francis	This place needs dusting!
Jimmy	You have a visitor
Francis	A visitor? Who?
Jimmy	A young lady. A pretty young lady.
Francis	Well I'd be damned
Jimmy	Yes, she's acting in the most peculiar manner. Wouldn't say what her reasons for calling upon you were, but insisted that she must! I would've sent her away if she hadn't seemed quite so desperate.

Francis   What did you tell her?

Jimmy   I told her I'd see whether you were ready to take visitors.

Francis   Jimmy I specifically told you not to reveal my presence in the house before consulting me!

Jimmy   Very well...sir

Jimmy starts to leave

Francis   Wait! Jimmy!

Jimmy   What is it now, sir?

Francis   I'm not wearing any trousers!

Pause

Jimmy   So you're not.

Francis   Well, I can't receive a lady in this fashion, can I?

Jimmy   No, I suppose not.

Francis   Quick give me yours!

Jimmy   But/

Francis   No buts! And don't you want to prove your loyalty to me?

Jimmy   Yes but/

Francis   Go on then.

There's an awkward and clumsy attempt to exchange clothing. Nothing quite fits and they can't seem to put the clothes on the right way around. After this struggle, Francis ends up only in his underwear. Jimmy is back in his bellboy outfit.

Jimmy   I'll send her up

Francis   Perfect

Jimmy leaves

Francis   *(shouting after Jimmy!)* What is her name?

But Jimmy has already left the room

Francis   *(to himself)* Theresa

He lies down on the chair and pulls out a cigarette from behind his ear. A young woman enters the room. She is carrying a camera.
She starts to take photos of him. He very happily poses for her.

Francis   Come here

She walks towards him and he takes her in his arm and kisses her. He grabs the camera

Francis   Sit down

He starts to click away on the camera

Francis   You are beautiful.

Theresa   Stop it!

Francis   It is true. You're the most beautiful woman
                             in the world

Theresa	Don't be silly.
Francis	I've seen many women in my life. From all corners of the world.
Theresa	If you had, you wouldn't say I was the most beautiful.
Francis	Would I lie to you?
Theresa	I don't know.
Francis	I don't lie my dear. It's not part of my make up

Pause

Francis	Although…I think you'd be even more beautiful if *(he goes over to her and pulls her blouse down over her shoulder)*

He takes a few more photos.
And maybe (he hitches her skirt up to reveal her thigh)

Pause

Theresa	Frank?
Francis	Yes, my dear

Pause

Francis	What is it?
Theresa	Um…Are you happy Frank?

Frank   Sure.

Theresa   I...

Francis   When I'm with you. Are you not?

Theresa   Of course I am Frank, I love you.

Francis   I love you too, my dear

Pause

She sits down on his lap

Francis   Close your eyes

Theresa   What? Why?

Francis   Just do what I say

She does.

He takes a few more photos.

Francis   (*laughs*) Now imagine the opposite. Imagine
                   we're somewhere completely different.
                   Imagine the sun beaming on your face

Theresa   Mmm

Francis   How does it feel?

Theresa   Warm? And lovely.

Francis   What do you see?

Theresa	A beach.
Francis	Where?
Theresa	On a beautiful island surrounded by turquoise-coloured waters.
Francis	Who's there?
Theresa	You and me…and a nice old man in a straw hat and dungarees handing us ripe fruit from the trees…and he speaks in the most peculiar accent *(giggles)*

Pause

Francis	What if I told you I know that beach, that I know that island?
Theresa	I'd say stop teasing me!
Francis	I do. I know exactly where that is! And we're going!
Theresa	Frank/
Francis	Tobago!
Theresa	Where?
Francis	The island of Tobago. In the West Indian Sea!
Theresa	I don't understand
Francis	There's a way for us both to leave this cold and damp place. A way that we can get to Tobago. But you need to listen to me.

Theresa	I am.
Francis	There's something you need to do for me first. For us. I'm going to give you the address to a café called the Rainbow Café, there you'll have to pick something up for me. For us. It's very valuable, so you must be very careful.
Theresa	What is it?
Francis	And you mustn't ask any questions. The less you know the better. For now. So, tomorrow you'll head down to the Rainbow Café. At the far right of the counter you'll ask for Maggie, the Princess of Tobago. And don't forget to curtsey, she is royalty after all.
Theresa	Frank I/
Francis	Maggie, the Princess of Tobago. Please pay attention; you must remember all of this. Now her highness will show you to a door at the back of the building. The door has a bell but you mustn't use it. Instead knock five times. Quietly. Like this. . .
	Knock, knock, knock, knock, knock
Francis	Once inside you'll be met by a young boy.
Theresa	And what is his name?
Francis	That's not important! He's just a boy. Call him "boy" if you so wish. He won't take offence. But you must tell him that you are there on behalf of Francis.

Theresa	Francis?
Francis	What did I tell you about asking too many questions? Now, the boy will give you a box. Take the box home. Then the next day before dawn you'll head down to the harbour. At the western pier you'll meet a man. And you'll give him the box in exchange for another box.
Theresa	How will I know which man?
Francis	You'll recognise him.
Theresa	How?
Francis	Because... he'll be wearing a straw hat and dungarees. Now, you give him the box, and he'll give you another one and a ticket to go on the boat.
Theresa	Boat?
Francis	The one that will take us to the West Indian Sea!

She looks at him in astonishment

Theresa	And yours? Don't we need two tickets?
Francis	Don't worry about me. I'll meet you on the boat.
Theresa	Oh I don't know, Frank.
Francis	There's no time for doubt.

He kisses her

Francis   So will you remember?

Theresa   Yes I think so…The Rainbow café… Maggie… remember to curtsey…knock, knock, knock, knock, knock…

Francis   Good. And remember to knock as quietly as you can.

Theresa   Are you sure about all of this?

Francis   As sure as the waters are turquoise around Tobago!

Theresa   Frank I/

Francis   Go on. Oh and here's the address for the Rainbow café, there's no time to talk. Besides we'll have all the time in the world to talk later.

Theresa   I love you, Frank.

She leaves

Francis stands up on the chair again and turns his back…he starts to sing a song. Francis has a beautiful voice.

Sunset and evening star,
And one clear call for me!
And may there be no moaning of the bar
When I put out to sea.

But such a tide as moving seems asleep,
Too full for sound and foam.
When that which drew from the boundless deep
Turns again home.

Twilight and evening bell,
And after that the dark!
And may there be no sadness of farewell
When I embark.

For, though from out our bourne of time and place
The flood may bear me far,
I hope to see my Pilot face to face
When I have crossed the bar.

(Crossing the Bar lyrics by by Alfred, Lord Tennyson)

Francis having this whole time held on to his cigarette, stubs it on the floor and starts pacing around the room.

After a while a sorry looking man wearing a straw hat and dungarees enters the room. He's carrying a wooden box

Francis   What took you so long? You're late!

Douglas   *(speaking in a "funny accent")* I'm sorry I came as fast as I could. But many things happened on the . . .

Francis   Give me that! And you can drop the accent.
Douglas hands him the box

Francis has a quick peek at what's inside then puts it under the chair.

Francis   Good. And I'm sorry about the dungarees.

Douglas   It is in the middle of winter. Damn cold out there by the harbour.

Francis   It's what the girl wanted.

Douglas   Francis I/

Francis	Francis who?
Douglas	I'm sorry
Francis	Do you see a Francis in here? Do you? Oh hold on, let's have a look (he starts to mock search around the room) Francis? Helloooo Francis? You there? Francis? little sissy boy where are you hiding? Hello?
	How strange…No Francis…
Douglas	I'm sorry Frank I just/
Francis	I bet you are. Look at you!
Douglas	Yes… I do apologise.
Francis	Don't you worry.
Douglas	But I really am so/
Francis	Stop that, you look pathetic. And you're starting to bore me with your apologies. I don't like being bored.
Douglas	Sorry. Oh. Yes I will. But I was wondering/
Francis	Oh hold on my dear Douglas, before you ask me anything I have a question for you!
Douglas	Yes Frank.
Francis	Where's the rest?
Douglas	The rest?

Francis	Yes you sorry excuse for a man. The Rest! Or are you telling me that the buggers in the clubs are stuffing their pipes with opium for free!?
Douglas	I/
Francis	The money!
Douglas	Yes

Douglas hands Francis a wad of notes

Francis	This is for you my friend

He hands him a single note

Douglas	I thought…I thought we said ten percent.
Francis	We did. But then you were late. There's always a fine for being late. Make sure you're not next time and you'll get your ten percent.
Douglas	Thank you Frank
Francis	You are most welcome my friend.

Douglas starts to leave

Francis	*(as he is counting the money)* And the girl?
Douglas	What about her?
Francis	She get on the boat?
Douglas	Yes she did.

Francis   Very well.

Douglas   Although with what was in the box I wouldn't
                         be certain she reaches shore the other end /

Francis   Don't be so pessimistic my dear friend. Don't
                         you know that the world is a beautiful place?
                         And beautiful things happen in it. You just
                         need to want it.

Douglas   I hope you're right.

Douglas leaves

Francis   Douglas!

But Douglas is already gone

*Francis who has been in only his underwear this whole time, picks up the blanket
and wraps it around himself. His youthful ways start to wear off – he looks tired…*

He hums a few notes of "Crossing the Bar"

Enter Jimmy

He walks over to him

Jimmy   Francis?

Francis   Oh Jimmy, where have you been? I thought
                         you'd never come back.

Francis   I'm tired, Jimmy.

Jimmy   You need to rest, Francis

Francis   I don't fancy a rest

Jimmy	What have we said about fancies?

Pause

Jimmy	What have you told me about fancies?
Francis	A fancy is not a want or a need. It is nothing…
Jimmy	Exactly.
Francis	I don't want to rest!
Jimmy	I think maybe you ought to.
Francis	Please Jimmy!
Jimmy	Very well.

Jimmy takes a very small wooden box out of his pocket opens it and lets Francis take a little sniff from it.

Francis	Jimmy?
Jimmy	Yes, Francis?
Francis	Do you hate me?

Pause

Jimmy	Of course not, Francis.

Long pause

Francis	Forgive me, I can be so cruel. So cruel. I can't help it. I've tried not to…But every time I was on the cusp of goodness, at every junction of kindness…I swerved into the curve of

nastiness…the vowels and consonants rested on a velvet tongue…but when they left my lips they came out full of thorns and spite…

Jimmy   There, there…

Francis   And when I was dealt love… I played a bluff…Ha!

Jimmy   Now don't be so harsh on yourself.

Pause

Francis   I always won though. I kept winning! The best poker face in the country!

Jimmy   Hush now.

Francis   Oh love and kindness sure makes people stupid! I was just there to feast on the leftovers of their foolishness! Right, Jimmy? Look around you! Look where we are! This house! Now the master of all of this! Had it not been for my wicked ways none of this would be in front of us! Maybe if people weren't such naïve mugs I wouldn't be such a horrible devil!

Jimmy   You do not mean what you say

Francis   Oh I sure do! What has anyone ever done for me? Huh?

A loud bang on the door interrupts them. This time Jimmy does not hesitate. He goes straight for the door

Francis   Jimmy! JIMMY!

Pause

Francis   Damn you!

He brings out the money again. Smells it. He walks around the room. He doesn't notice, but Sister Janet has entered the room again. She is carrying a suitcase. She observes him for a while.

Sister Janet   I see you haven't found your trousers...

He turns around

You've grown. I can see that. But surely there are trousers made in sizes suited for grown men.

Francis   You don't/

Sister Janet   You? Ah, yes of course! What would Sister Janet know? Sister Janet has never worn trousers in her life! Stupid Sister Janet...

Francis   I um/

Sister Janet   Tell me Francis, did you find what you were looking for?

Francis   You have a... are you leaving?

Sister Janet   Yes. Missionary. Caribbean islands. The boat leaves in a few hours...

Francis   Don't leave

Sister Janet   I thought I'd come by to say my goodbyes. To see how you were Francis. I think of you often. I can see that you're doing very well.

She refers to the money in his hands

He embarrassingly tries to hide the money. In a pocket. Or a hat. But alas he is almost stark naked.

He gives her a cigarette and lights it for her

Pause

Sister Janet   … I said life was beautiful. I never said it was easy. If it was, then we would not be given it. Nothing is given for free. The cost is big. Sometimes so big that you can't see past it. But behind that mountain lies the pay off. And lord knows it's sweet. On the other side is nectar so delicious it's almost frightening to taste. But one has to climb that hill. One must endure that gravel road. And then one should be brave enough to stick one's tongue out to receive. Because sometimes it's awfully bitter. And sometimes the taste is as sour as a green citrus fruit.

Pause

You see Francis. You seem to think it's sweet like molasses. You chase after a taste that is syrupy. But when you hunt for things treacle-like, you'll end up caught in your own sticky trap.

No, Francis It is salty. Salty like the vast ocean... Oh you'll beg for that brine...and you'll know in that moment that to live, is to be free. And freedom is the sweetest taste of all!

Francis   Why are you telling me all of this? You don't care

Sister Janet	Because Francis, I hope you get to taste it one day. Because I know that you have something that keeps you imprisoned…Goodbye Francis.

She leaves

Enter Jimmy

Francis	Jimmy! Don't you find it odd? All these people/
Jimmy	Francis, I'm afraid I'm going to have to interrupt you. We have some more pressing matters at hand.
Francis	I/
Jimmy	The woman is back. This time with two police officers at the door. And they've certainly brought their hatches.
Francis	Tell them to bugger off
Jimmy	I don't think they'll take very kindly to that.
Francis	What do I care?

Loud banging on the door starts again. The music Francis sang earlier swells…

Jimmy	Francis, now would be a good time to tell me. I can't help you if you won't let me. Please, Francis. Why are the police here?
Francis	I don't know!
Jimmy	Yes you do, Francis. And you need to tell. They'll break the door down now any minute

The loud banging continues

Francis Just let them take me away

Jimmy No, Francis I won't let them do that! Just tell me, I promise I'll make sure you won't get into any trouble!

Francis I don't want to/

Jimmy Now Francis!

Francis Stupid Trousers! Stupid Sister Janet!

Jimmy Francis! Quick!

Francis jumps out of the chair and grabs the box from under it. Jimmy snatches it from his hands.

Jimmy Well done, Francis.

Francis What happens now?

Pause

He leaves

The banging continues.

Francis collapses into the chair.

And the banging continues. And continues . . .

UNDER WOOD ISLAND

BY HESTER KENT

This was an idea that came out of two separate stories from two different care centres. I was interested in the juxtaposition between each of the protagonists: one, a "property tycoon", the other a "hippy"; both searching for pleasure; one, from money; the other, from "cakes with forbidden substances". The essence of the story was to capture the free loving spirit of eternal youth, maintained beautifully by another gentleman's wishes to be half man, half bird: Birdman.

Story created by those from the Phoenix Centre and Claydon House

Character List
Ivan Wood/Birdman: Owner of Wood Island. Twenties
Hugh G Under: Property Tycoon. Thirties
Judy: Hippy. Early-mid twenties
Baker: Thirties

Set/Place
Utopian islands near Dover Castle
1960s

Scene I

*Scenic viewpoint on top of mountain peak. Dover Castle is seen on the
neighbouring island. A man sits alone with easel, painting the wild birds
flying overhead. He gets shat on repeatedly. First, a small splattering,
until his whole canvas is covered. He loses his patience and throws his
paintbrush down. This has happened far too many times. Surely, there
must be a solution.*

*Later that morning. Scenic viewpoint on top of mountain peak on a
remote island. The same man is sat in a pair of wings. He gets out his
paintbrush and begins to paint the wild birds overhead. A bird shits, but
it misses him (by a narrow margin, landing on the grass next to him).
This happens two times but no shit on man. Success.*

*A well to do gentleman comes over the peak. He sets his little fold away
stool out. He hears the sound of the birds overhead. He looks up. He is
shat on. He takes off his hat and proceeds to clean it with a handkerchief.*

Hugh Under	What a view. Did you ever see one quite like it?
Ivan Wood	Yeah. There.
Hugh Under	Hugh G. Under
Ivan Wood	Ivan Wood
Hugh Under	I'm the proprietor of Dover Castle. You may also know me from such literary titles as: 'They're mad. We're all mad. So that makes us equal' and 'If Alan Sugar were a property tycoon in Utopia'. I'm quite huge.

Ivan Wood	I can't read.
Hugh Under	Oh come now. You're being modest. The island people say you're a remarkable man. How else would a man of your stature come to acquire their own beautiful island. They say this is a special place, Mr Wood, with very special properties
Ivan Wood	Yeah. I know. I live here
Hugh Under	You inherited it from your late father, isn't that right, Mr Wood?
Ivan Wood	If you say so
Hugh Under	A truly remarkable story. A fishmonger no less. And what a catch to net a place like this. I'm dying to know his secret
Ivan Wood	No
Hugh Under	I'll kill you for it. Ha, ha, ha, ha. Joking. But, really, I could, I'm that huge. *(Referring to IVAN WOOD's painting).* An artist too. Your father had a good dabble with the paints, didn't he? In fact, one of his most famous pieces hangs in my castle: *'The Mermaid and the Naked Maraca Dancer'*
Ivan Wood	Where'd you get that?
Hugh Under	Wood Island is not the only special island here, Mr Wood
Ivan Wood	I paint birds

Hugh Under	Excellent. Good for you.
Ivan Wood	You've got bird poo on you
Hugh Under	Yes, well, they're quite tame for wild birds. You see, if I owned Wood Island, Mr Wood, I would set up a bird sanctuary. Sorry, I meant cage.
Ivan Wood	They're on a diet of grass. They're so high you haven't a hope in hell of catchin' one. Doesn't do much for their intestines
Hugh Under	Grass?
Ivan Wood	It's all about the grass here
Hugh Under	Tell me friend, why do the island people call you 'Birdman'?
Ivan Wood	Cos I'm their master. And this island, is a herb shop
Hugh Under	Herb shop? I was under the impression this was an island, Mr Wood. Care to elaborate
Ivan Wood	Evaporate?
Hugh Under	Hm. Smarter than I thought. I'm going to get straight to the point, Wood. I'm buying this island and you're selling it to me. Understood?

A bird shits on HUGH UNDER's hat. Again.

Ivan Wood	No one's havin' this island except me, Judy, and the baker

Hugh Under   I'm Hugh G. Under. I've just closed a three trillion pound deal on every island you see

Ivan Wood   You're not havin' Wood Island. End of.

Another bird shits on HUGH UNDER

Ivan Wood   How'd you get past the gates anyway?

Hugh Under   They were wide open, Mr Wood. Perhaps you need to reconsider your security

Ivan Wood   JUDY

Hugh Under   Give me this island

Ivan Wood   No

Hugh Under   Give it to me or else

Ivan Wood   No

Hugh Under   I have one billion pounds right here in my pocket to convince you otherwise

Ivan Wood   What in them pockets?

Hugh Under   I have a blank cheque for one billion pounds

Ivan Wood   You shouldn't carry that in your pocket. Especially not round here

Hugh Under   Think of all the easels you could buy. Mahogany easels

Ivan Wood   I hate mahogany

Hugh Under   Wings. You could buy huge wings

Ivan Wood   The birds give me wings

A bird shits on HUGH UNDER

IVAN WOOD hands him a pair of wings

Ivan Wood   These might help

Hugh Under   They're fairy wings

Ivan Wood   Yeah. There's only one Birdman. And that's me

A bird is heard squawking overhead

Ivan Wood   I'd put 'em on if I were you

HUGH UNDER puts on the fairy wings

Ivan Wood   See that's the thing, Mr Under. Money don't mean anything to these 'ere birds. You want this island, you'll 'ave to get past them first.

Hugh Under   I'll have them eating out of my hand like a kangaroo eating fruit from a bush.

Ivan Wood   The only kangaroos you'll see eating any bush here, are hallucinogenic ones.

Hugh Under   Take the bloody birds, I don't care. I'm going to build a hotel, Mr Wood. The biggest, shiniest most opulent, ridiculously overpriced hotel you can imagine. There'll be no extra pillows. No shower caps. No complimentary bathrobes for people like you to steal. Just a mini bar, and some fancy-looking, but terrible, artwork. *(He looks at Ivan's painting)*. That would do perfectly. I know about the ship

Ivan Wood   What do you know?

Hugh Under   That an old wooden ship lies under Wood Island and no one knows about it, until now. And its treasure is worth having, is it not, Mr Wood?

Ivan Wood   You can't have that ship

Hugh Under   *(laughs)* one billion pounds, Mr Wood. That's my final offer

Ivan Wood   Or what?

Hugh Under   Or…I'll tell Judy and your baker that you've got vaults in that ship worth zillions of pounds

Ivan Wood   How do you know that they don't know about the vaults? They might know what you don't know but think you know, that I know

Hugh Under   WHAT

Ivan Wood   Goodbye, Mr Under

HUGH UNDER stands up and removes his fairy wings

Hugh Under   I want you gone by tomorrow morning

A bird shits on HUGH UNDER, then another, then another, until he is bombarded and has no choice but to walk away

Scene 2

Wood Island gates. A gate keeper stands guard. It is a woman in a floral apron. The front pocket of her apron is stuffed full of cake.

Hugh Under   Let me off this island

Baker   No

Hugh Under   Excuse me, I said

Baker   No

Hugh Under   STAND ASIDE

Baker   NO

Hugh Under   Who's your superior?

Baker   Judy

Hugh Under   Right. Well get Judy here; tell her I want a word

Baker   JUDY

JUDY floats on in a hippy scarf

Judy   Hello

Hugh Under   OPEN THIS GATE

Judy   Of course. But you can't leave without having a piece of cake first

Hugh Under   Do you know who I am?

Baker   No

Judy   Yes, we know who you are, Mr Hugh. G. Under.
                We hope you enjoyed your time on Wood Island

Baker   Yes

Judy   Do you like a good time?

Hugh Under I...Pardon?

Baker   I made cake

Hugh Under What sort of cake?

Judy   It's not a sponge

Baker   Brownie

Judy   Brownie?

Hugh Under That's very kind of you, but I don't accept
                cake from strange women

Judy   This is not just any cake, Mr Under. This is a
                Wood Island cake. We cannot open this gate
                until you take this cake off our hands. So
                you see you need to eat the cake

Baker   Brownie

Judy   She baked it

HUGH UNDER takes the cake and eats it

Hugh Under MMMM. That's delicious.

Baker   Forbidden

Judy	Forbidden delicious

They both start giggling like two school girls

Baker	HASH CAKE
Hugh Under	I think I should go. My castle is waiting
Judy	We're just having a bit of fun, Hugh. You might start feeling crazy and want to start laughing. Who doesn't like to laugh?

BAKER laughs

JUDY laughs

Indian music plays distantly and gets louder

Judy	Can you hear the music yet?
Hugh Under	What music?
Baker	I hear the music
Judy	The music, Mr Under, can you hear the music?
Hugh Under	This is madness, I...I...can hear the music

JUDY starts doing Indian dancing

BAKER starts dancing

Hugh Under	I can't stop my feet moving. Now my hips are going. My arms. WHAT'S HAPPENING TO MY ARMS?

HUGH UNDER starts dancing too. He doesn't notice *the cheque fall out of his pocket*

Judy   *(to Baker)* Get the wings

BAKER gets bird wings and puts them on HUGH UNDER. BAKER hands JUDY her wings and BAKER puts on hers

Judy   Now you are one of us

Hugh Under   I'm one of you. FLY LITTLE BIRDIES.
                              HIGH, HIGH, HIGH IN THE SKY. Where's
                              Birdman? BIRDMAN

Judy   BIRDMAN

Baker   BIRDMAN

HUGH UNDER heads towards the mountain peak where BIRDMAN is. Then he gets an idea

Hugh Under   Want to come to a festival?

Judy   I'm going along with you

Baker   *(to Judy)* You look nice, very pretty

Judy   HASH CAKE

Hugh Under   HASH CAKE

Baker   HASH. CAKE.

Judy   It's a lovely day, let's enjoy ourselves

Baker   It's nice here

Hugh Under WE'RE GOING TO A FESTIVAL.

Judy Where?

Baker I can't see one

Hugh Under On my island. Do you want to go?

Baker They say the Beatles might be there

Judy I'd love to go

Hugh Under I'm not sure if The Beatles...sod it . . . THE BEATLES ARE GOING TO BE THERE

Baker It would be great if you could dance with The Beatles

Judy I want to dance with The Beatles

Hugh Under SO DO I

They all cheer

The Beatles can be heard in the background. They stop to listen and can hardly believe their ears

Hugh Under THE BEATLES ARE THERE

They all run from the gate and towards the festival

BAKER runs back to the gate and hugs it

Baker Bye gate

BAKER exits

IVAN WOOD has come down from the hilltop, paintbrush in hand, palette in the other

Ivan Wood   Guys?

IVAN WOOD spots a small, folded piece of paper on the ground. He opens it up. It is a blank cheque to the amount of one billion pounds.

He pulls out a pen and writes his name on the payable to line

Ivan Wood   Payable to Ivan Wood; A.K.A Birdman.

Here Comes the Sun by The Beatles plays as he exits

THE DEAD ZONE

BY ALEXANDER MOSCHOS

This was a phase penned by one of the residents we met at Claydon House, Lewes. It was how she described her difficulties to tell the time. That paired with some wonderful stories about the ocean and plenty of bicycles from The Phoenix Centre, Lewes. That's how the play became the story of a girl obsessed with a cycling man.

Woman

Sometimes I speak to myself from the future. Or if it is me speaking to myself from the past…It is difficult to know. But it is never a conversation…So it must be one or the other.

I assure myself that life is good and that I am gay and jolly. But it is easy to lie to oneself when there is so much time in between unaccounted for.

Time is such a dreary thing. Especially now! It is summer. And the days feel very long and tedious!

On the last day of school before the summer holidays, we all stood in front of the main brick building, where the older children have their classes and the headmaster's office is and sang songs to a crowd of parents. The day before, our teacher had made the whole class go outside the school grounds to pick flowers from the meadow to make garlands that we would wear in our hair for the performance. Our teacher, who is a very silly woman, seemed overcome with excitement at the thought of us all in our best clothes and wilted flowers in our hair.

I did not put the flowers in my hair and I wore the same dress I had worn the day before.

And I didn't sing either. I just looked out at the horde of bored parents. Wishing I was somewhere else. I had wished myself away many times before. But always remained exactly where I was. Why

PLAYS

I thought it would work this time. I do not know.

But suddenly there was a loud shriek followed by the screaming of a young child! Jens Larsson's little sister was standing right there at the front of the crowd and there was blood gushing from her nose. Mrs Larsson was hysterical and the hysteria spread like wildfire and sure enough, within seconds the singing had stopped. The crowds dispersed and Jen's little sister was carried away crying and covered in blood.

Time has a way of speeding up. Like when a crowd of people run in panic. A bit like when you stick a twig in an ant nest. But it can also slow down. Like when blood hits the white satin dress of a small child. The way the drops run down the fabric like dewdrops on a spider web.

And sometimes you get what you wish for.

That all seems like such a long time ago now. The summer days go on forever. For all I know that day at school when Jen's little sister almost bled to death and everyone, apart from myself, wore flowers in their hair could've been years ago.

That's the thing about time. It's all about before and after. You need events, sort of like yardsticks, to tell one time from another… but what of the time in between when nothing happens? How does one measure that?… My father gave me a wristwatch for my ninth birthday but I do not wear it during the summer months because my skin under the leather strap gets all sweaty and sticky, and I do not like to be moist.

We live in an old wooden house on the cliffs looking out over the ocean. When I say "we", I mean myself, my mother and my father. It is a very small house and we never have any visitors. There's only one bedroom in the house and the dining room is for eating so I sleep in the kitchen. It is light outside when I fall asleep and still light when I wake up. So in a way it is as if the days never really end…or start.

At the edges of the cliffs the waves roll in, they roll out….yet time stands still.

And that takes me to the event. The cliffs. That's where I first saw him. There on the cliffs.

He was lying there on the rocks next to his bicycle. Sprawled out with his arms crossed behind his head. He'd been for a swim. I could tell because his hair was still damp. The water had made his wavy hair look a little darker in places than it probably was. Like the sand on a beach. Closer to his head it was an ashy grey. Towards the ends a golden yellow.

The heat from the sun had dried out the last droplets of the salty ocean water on his skin. And all that remained were the crystallised minerals…

In that late evening sun, the crystals shone… like how I imagine a goldmine somewhere in Africa would do.

A slight chill had arrived in the air and it made the small hairs on his body stand up straight. Shooting out from his skin like the first little shoots of the crocus in springtime. Every tiny cell on his skin on alert.

It was as if my eyes turned into a microscope, just like the ones we use in biology class to look at tiny fungi and bacteria. Seeing every detail of his bronzed body magnified a million times. Or do I mean a telescope? Because somehow it was as if I was looking at him from very far away. Not just a few feet, but light years rather. On a planet, somewhere in another universe where he was very small and the space around him an eternal vacuum.

I have to sit next to Louise in biology class. Louise Heim, Louise with her sweaty pinkish skin and frizzy hair. I hate Louise. I wish there was a world where I did not have to endure her sour stench and dry curls. But no-one else wants to sit with me. And so I have to.

I hate Louise. Father tells me I should not hate. Because to hate is a sin. But I do. And there is so much to hate. So much of Louise. So much excess.

If there was a little less of her. Maybe I would not hate so much. But my feelings for Louise are dull, like the thud on a wall in a room at the other end of the house.

The feelings that struck me whilst watching him were of a different nature. Sharper somehow. Feelings that excited and terrified me. They crawled right under my skin. From the tips of my toes straight through my body towards the top of my head where I could feel them tingle. Fever-like.

Violent thoughts. Thoughts that I had not had before.

To smother him. Just a little

Just so he'd feel a bit of pressure in his chest. That chest that seemed to breathe so freely. Just a tiny bit.

To make him gasp for air.

Suddenly, the man stood up. I had not noticed that he was not wearing any clothes. He was tall and the muscles on his body lean and tight. A pair of shorts had been lying beside him to dry on the rocks. He put them on. Looked around. I, who was not sure quite where I was. How close to him I was, sat very still. He picked up his bike and walked away.

I wanted to follow him. But if I moved, he would see me. And although I was tall for my age, he was taller. One of his steps equalled at least two and a half of my own. Either way, by the time he got to the road he'd get on his bike and I wouldn't be able to keep up.

I will find him. Not today. Tomorrow. These things need to be planned.

It is not ideal to have Louise with me. She is slow. She is stupid. She revolts me... But... I need an accomplice. To be by oneself will seem suspicious.

Also Louise has a bicycle. Or two rather. Louise has a lot of things because she is from a wealthy family. Her father is a lawyer. A short pig-like man with a squeaky voice. Father says Louise's father is a moral-less man. Lawyers lie. To lie is another sin and therefore Mr Heim is a sinner.

Still he is rich. Rich enough to buy Louise two bicycles. And I need one. So that's that.

Later that evening I walk down the gravel path away from our house onto the main road. I need to pay the Heims a visit.

Plans like these need to be delivered in person. Whispered even… and we do not have a telephone so I have no other choice. Writing a note is too risky. Someone else might read it and telling Louise is already one person too many to tell.

The Heim house has a door knocker in the shape of a pig's foot. This is meant to be both funny and decorative. It is neither.

Mr Heim comes to the door. Although he is much older than myself. I feel as though I'm looking down on him.

"Is Louise home?" I ask

"Well hello to you too," he laughs.

I'm staring right down into his nostrils.

"May I speak to Louise, please?"

"You're a very odd young girl"

"We've just sat down for dinner, you're more than welcome to join us."

"No, thanks"

"A bit of meat on those bones wouldn't do you any harm.

Maybe Mr Heim thinks I ought to be more like Louise.

"May I have a word with Louise?"

"Ha ha, absolutely ... Yes, you may. You sure are strange"

When Louise comes to the door she has her mouth full of food. I'm not sure. But it looks like sausage and potatoes.

"Hi. We're in the middle of dinner. Want to join? Please do! It's sausage Thursday! "

It all makes sense now.

"No thanks, I need to ask you for a favour"

"Are you sure? About sausage Thursday I mean?"

"Listen, I need your help."

"With what?"

"First, I need to borrow your bicycle"

"For what?"

"A mission"

"A mission?"

"Yes and I want you to come with me."

"YES!"

"You can't tell anyone about it. I'll meet you here tomorrow morning."

"Ooooh, a secret mission!"

"Yes."

"We're spies!"

"Just meet me here tomorrow morning."

"But what . . .

I'm already running. I run all the way home. I do not usually run. But I'm eager to get to bed. I must be well rested. That night I dreamt of volcanoes and snakes.

The next day when I arrive at the Heims' Louise is already waiting outside. She is wearing a woollen blazer, a little cape, and a flat cap.

"I wasn't sure what a spy would wear, so I thought I'd be a detective instead.

It is a warm summer's morning and Louise is already sweating.

"Oh and look, I brought this."

She picks out a magnifying glass from her pocket.

"I also brought some salami sandwiches and a couple of boiled eggs. In case we get hungry"

Usually all of this would've annoyed me. But today I appreciate Louise's commitment. It is still stupid to wear wool in the middle of summer and salami makes me nauseous. But today I don't care, today Louise is my partner and I like her.

We wait for him at the end of the path that leads to my house and further on; the cliffs. I figure that he is a man of routines, he'll have been for his afternoon swim. He should be on his way back any minute.

We're hiding behind some bushes so that he won't see us. And sure enough. There he is rolling down the hill.

"SHH"

Once he's turned onto the main road we jump out from behind the bushes and get on our bikes.

"Quick"

"He's real fast"

Louise is right. He is. I imagine he's a professional cyclist. There is determination in his pedalling...

Now he's riding without holding onto the handlebar. His arms are outstretched like wings and his blond hair is blowing in the wind.

I hate and love him in equal measures.

All of a sudden, he swerves into one of the side streets

"OOH, he's on his way to the pub!"

This does not fit the profile. A professional cyclist would not spend time with the drunkards in that horrible place.

"Should we follow him inside?"

"No, that will look suspicious,"

We position ourselves by the side of the building where we can watch him through one of the stained-glass windows. Blue and red stained. Four squares. Louise watches him in blue. I see him in red. He keeps looking at a clock right above the barmaid's head. He is waiting for someone.

"I'm hungry. Do you want your sandwich?"

I do not.

"Well I'm going to have mine now. I'll save the egg for later, this mission might take some time, don't you think?"

He orders another drink.

"Spying sure is good for one's appetite."

A young woman joins him. They sit in silence. Their lips are not moving – he finishes his drink and they get up to leave. I can hear the door open at the front of the building. And laughter.

We wait for a short moment then we get back on our bicycles.

She is sitting on the handlebar. This time his hands are firmly gripped on them. They're on their way back to the cliffs. She is still laughing.

I never laugh.

It is mysterious how you can watch someone's every move, every turn and for them not to see you at all. Not even once.

We follow them back up the path past my house. He carries his bicycle over one shoulder and holds her hand with the other. He's leading her to the same spot I'd seen him the day before.

She is sitting between his legs and is resting her head on his chest. He is playing with her hair and kisses her neck. She giggles. She looks happy. He reaches into his pocket and picks out a little box. Puts it in front of her and opens it. The rays of the sun reflect on the object inside and sends beams of light across the cliffs. One hits me right in the eye, almost blinding me.

It is a ring. She turns around and looks at it with shock and excitement. Her hands over her mouth. Then she stretches the left one towards him and he puts the ring on it.

"He's proposing!"

"Shh!"

"Sorry….did you want your sandwich? Cause if you don't I'll have it. I don't really like egg."

"Yes, you can have it, just be quiet."

Just as I'd started to like her, my old feelings for Louise have started to brew again.

They're embracing each other. Laughing and kissing. She is

laying on top of him. He's unzipped her dress and she stands up and removes it completely.

Salami makes me nauseous.

She's gotten down on her knees in front of him, unbuckles his belt and kisses him. He grabs hold of her and turns her onto her back and gets on top of her. He pulls down his trousers and unbuttons his shirt.

Louise starts to giggle nervously. I elbow her to make her stop. "OUCH!"

She can't stop giggling. He's standing in front of her and removes his underwear.

I can hear Louise clumsily running away. Down the cliffs, back towards where we left the bicycles. But I don't look away.

I keep my eyes on him.

She's left the half-eaten sandwich. I can smell it.

He's laying on top of her. And it becomes hard to tell where she starts and where he ends. They are entwined; like snakes in brumation. But they are not still. They move and change position. The sun has started to set and it casts an orange and red light over their naked bodies like two metals melting and merging in a ferocious fire. Tiny explosions of bubbling magma. Time, it seemed, was speeding up and slowing down at the same time.

There's a loud ringing in my ears like an air raid siren.

Sparks fly off the puddle of sweat and skin and dying when it hits the dark cliffs. It is coming to an end. The molten rock solidifies in a heap of heavy breaths. He's rolled away from her now.

The siren has gone quiet. The sun has set and it is dark. She puts her dress on and starts to walk away…

What happened next, I'm not sure of. My acute spying eye had turned lazy. But I think he got up. Stumbled a little. Regained his balance and walked towards the edge of the cliff and dove into the dark ocean. I did not hear the sound of a splash when he hit the water. Just silence. Maybe he was not a cyclist but a diver? Divers might drink with the hollow-eyed men in the pub?

I lay on my back on the cliff staring up into the sky wishing I was somewhere else. Wishing myself away or just wishing I'd just turn into the lichen on the rock surface.

But maybe you only get one wish.

I did not wear flowers in my hair.

I do not wear a ring, a ring on my finger.

Sometimes I speak to myself from the future.

I assure myself that life is good and that I am gay and jolly. But it is easy to lie to oneself when there is so much time in between unaccounted for.

LOVE'S HERO

WRITTEN BY HESTER KENT

A touching story based on one woman's memory of swimming around West Brighton Pier. I saw the glint in her eye when she recalled the danger of it all, and how this closeness with mortality made her feel alive. I was struck at how the women in this care centre re-told their tussles with power as young women, and was humbled by their sense of humour when sharing this.

Character List
Erica – late twenties, swimmer. Brighton, born and bred
The Lifeguard – mid-twenties, male. Brighton, born and bred
Pete – Actor. Thirties. Originally from Brighton
Margaret – Twenties. Actress. From London

(The offstage voice of **Mother** can be played by the actress playing **Margaret**)

Time/Place
Brighton Pier
1980s

Scene 1

ERICA's bedroom. Brighton.
On the wall are posters of Olympic swimmers of that era, and medals adorn
her mantelpiece. Morning light streams through the window. ERICA jumps
out of bed and puts on her thick, colourful, rimmed glasses. She then takes
out her retainer and brushes her hair. A swimming cap is hanging off the
mirror. She puts this on. She then takes off her night dress to reveal a bathing
suit underneath. She takes a moment to check herself out in the mirror as the
swimmer persona is unveiled, before grabbing a tracksuit to put on.

We hear her mother calling offstage, 'BREAKFAST, ERICA'. ERICA
grabs her already packed swim bag with a sense of urgency and heads out,
passing the kitchen on the way, where mother is sat expectantly at the
dinner table. ERICA exits.

Scene 2
THE LIFEGUARD's bedroom. Brighton.

On the wall are posters of Brighton and Hove Lifeguard affiliation, and pictures of shipwrecks. There is a framed picture of him and his mother on the mantelpiece.

The sound of the alarm clock jolts him awake. He brushes his teeth, squeezing the very last drop of toothpaste from an empty tube, and splashes water on his face. It's cold. Too cold. He looks in the mirror and stares blankly, until the voice of his mother shouts up from the kitchen, 'BREAKFAST....YOU HAVEN'T SEEN MY MING VASE, HAVE YOU?'. He puts on his uniform, grabs his bag, and exits.

Scene 3

Brighton Pier. The morning sun shines more intensely as the early sea mist lifts. THE LIFEGUARD climbs up his high chair ready for a day's work and welcomes the glorious sunshine.

Erica   Lovely day for it

The Lifeguard   Morning

Erica performs her morning ritual. She takes off the tracksuit, glasses still on

The Lifeguard   Don't swim too close to the edge

Erica   You said that yesterday

The Lifeguard   And I'll keep saying it. It's for your own good, Miss. It's dangerous to swim round the pier

Erica   I know. Wonderful isn't it?

The Lifeguard   You have to respect the sea. There's no knowing what she'll do.

Erica   I respect the sea. I love her. She's the reason I'm such a good swimmer. I have nothing but respect for her.

The Lifeguard   Then why don't you swim further out? Why'd you have to hug the pier like that?

Erica   Oh I dunno. It's fun. Plus, you're here, so... you know. I'm Erica

She offers a hand up to THE LIFEGUARD. He awkwardly climbs down the high chair to accept it.

The Lifeguard Don't ladies swim in lidos?

Erica I've never thought about it. Sounds a bit boring, though.

The Lifeguard It's safer

Erica Yeah…that's not really my thing

The Lifeguard I'd have put you down as a lido swimmer

Erica Well. What can I say? You're wrong

The Lifeguard I used to work in a lido. It was really boring

Erica Do you swim?

The Lifeguard Of course I swim. I wouldn't be a very good lifeguard if I didn't swim

Erica When was the last time you went swimming?

The Lifeguard I only swim if I have to

Erica If you have to? But what if you just want to swim for fun?

The Lifeguard You've lost me

Erica You could throw yourself off that chair, right now, and dive into the sea, and feel the most alive you've probably felt in a long time. Don't you feel the urge to do that, once in a while? I have to swim every morning. As soon as I open my eyes in the morning, that's it, I have to get out. I have to get in the sea, and I have to go swimming

The Lifeguard   …and it has to be round this pier…

Erica   Yes, it does. You said it yourself; you have to respect the sea, there's no knowing what she'll do. Go too far out and you could find yourself in trouble.

The Lifeguard   And that's when I have to throw myself off my chair. It's not something I like to make a habit of

Erica   I've never seen you leave that chair. I'm starting to think your bottom's glued to it

The Lifeguard   I have swum in the sea. I used to swim every evening, in fact. Best time of the day, that is. Being in the sea as the sun's setting. I thought I could swim up to it and catch it before it sank.

Erica   And did you?

The Lifeguard   Too slow. I just kept going and going and it kept going and going. I thought I'm gonna swim to France at this rate. So then I'd eventually turn around and end up swimming back in the dark. I lost sight of the beach once. I'd drifted and then it got so dark I couldn't even make out the shore.

Erica   Swimming in the moonlight must've been beautiful. Maybe I should do that

The Lifeguard   Wasn't really thinking about the moon, to be honest; too busy fearing for my life

Erica   But didn't the moon make you feel safe? Mother Nature's very powerful

The Lifeguard   Yeah. She's also a woman; telling me how late it was and why wasn't I home already. It was the middle of the night. That's not a good time to be alone with Mother Nature, let me tell you

Erica   So what happened?

The Lifeguard   It got darker and darker and the current kept pulling me further and further away. Fortunately, it got light again and I saw the shore and never have I been happier to see Brighton Pier.

Erica   Oh, so you'd not gone that far out then

The Lifeguard   Only cos I managed to swim back. And it was cold. I could've died out there.

Erica   Well. I'm glad you didn't.

The Lifeguard   Me too. Had to walk back in my trunks; no towel; no shoes. Then of course when I'd got there, they'd gone. Someone'd 'ad 'em

Erica   Well. Least you weren't naked

The Lifeguard   I was practically naked. Luckily I live just up the road so I just walked home and sat in the bath until I was crinkly

Erica	I live up the road too.
The Lifeguard	No use to me now, is it. You live with your parents, then? I live with my mum. She's all right. She's a got a thing for Ming Vases. It's her dream to own a china shop one day so she just keeps collecting stuff then losing it. We're probably gonna need a bigger house. What does your dad think of you swimming round the pier?
Erica	You make it sound like it's illegal or something
The Lifeguard	Not illegal. But definitely reckless
Erica	Do you dare me to do a handstand off the pier?
The Lifeguard	No
Erica	Cos that would be reckless, wouldn't it
The Lifeguard	You could hit your head

ERICA does a handstand and lands on the edge of the pier. She looks over at THE LIFEGUARD to check he is watching, as she puts on a performance pretending to fall backwards, into the water. She recovers. Then falls. THE LIFEGUARD instinctively grabs his float and jumps off the edge to save her. He swims over to her and scoops her up in his arms. She begins laughing. She stops when she sees THE LIFEGUARD is not sharing the joke. She looks at him as he still holds her in his arms

Erica	YES. I got you in the water
The Lifeguard	…you needed

FOUND IN TRANSLATION

There is a moment before they break

The Lifeguard   I'm on lunch.

He leaves the water

Erica   SEE YOU LATER?

Scene 4

An artisan café on the seafront. MARGARET and PETE are sat on a table outside having their lunch. MARGARET has a basic soup of the day with bread. PETE is eating Eggs Benedict. He has his serviette tucked into his collar. He drips egg on his chin

Margaret   You've got egg on you

Pete   Have I?

Margaret   On your face

Pete   Where?

Margaret   Your chin

Pete starts using his hand to rub it off but misses each time

Margaret   It's still there

PETE has another failed attempt at locating the egg

Pete   Gone?

Margaret   Why don't you use your serviette?

Pete uses his serviette but fails again

Pete   Now?

Margaret   Come here

Margaret pulls his serviette from his hand and rubs off the egg

Margaret   Gone

Pete	Much obliged
Margaret	The bad news is, I couldn't afford to pay any other actors for the fight scene
Pete	Right. So the battle scene is you and me. That's it.
Margaret	...you did insist on Eggs Benedict...
Pete	Shall we practise?
Margaret	Have you got your props on you?
Pete	No. Sorry, I thought you had wardrobe on that
Margaret T	I am wardrobe. I couldn't afford to pay the assistant and unsurprisingly she didn't want to work for free, but she is going to supply her biodegradable confetti for the wedding scene, so every cloud, as they say. . .
Pete	Excellent. Some good news, at last. You know how much my eyes swell up around paper

Margaret stands up to reveal two plastic swords sticking out of her belt

Pete pulls an eye patch from his floral, velveteen waistcoat, while MARGARET hands him one of her plastic swords

They go into the first tableau of their scene. PETE launches his first parry to MARGARET

Margaret	Hang on a second

Pete	Oh. You've interrupted my flow, Margey. I told you not to do that. It'll take me at least 15 minutes to re-find my character
Margaret	You went forward on the wrong foot. You led with the right, when it should have been the left
Pete	Did I?
Margaret	From the top?

PETE makes the same mistake again. MARGARET stops

Margaret	You did it again
Pete	I think we've practised that enough now don't you?
Margaret	Right. Shall we head to our first location? This film won't shoot itself
Pete	Did we discuss the poem I wrote?
Margaret	No poem, Pete. Pirates don't speak in prose

Scene 5

Brighton Pier. Later that afternoon, ERICA is sunning herself on the pier, reading Treasure Island. THE LIFEGUARD comes back after his lunchbreak and climbs up his high chair. ERICA moves herself directly under his chair

Erica	Don't mind me. I need your shadow
The Lifeguard	Some of us have to dry off
Erica	Did you enjoy your lunch? What did you have?
The Lifeguard	A very soggy sandwich, thanks to you.

ERICA laughs. THE LIFEGUARD is not amused
ERICA suddenly feels unwelcome and moves her things back into the sun

THE LIFEGUARD lets her go

MARGARET and PETE arrive with their film set. ERICA's attention is turned towards them, as MARGARET takes off a robe to reveal a full coat of armour (homemade). PETE refuses to change from his favourite but non-piratey, velveteen, floral waistcoat. A little business ensues.

The action is broken with the sound of a telephone that rings out to answerphone. THE LIFEGUARD'S mother is heard as a recorded message: 'Son. It's the Ming Vase…are you there…?'

All our characters look perplexed, except for THE LIFEGUARD, who dutifully walks down from his high chair to take the call in the office, out of sight.

The business continues

ERICA sees the opportunity to climb up the high chair in THE

LIFEGUARD's absence, and takes up the loudspeaker. She directs this at
MARGARET and PETE

Erica   *(loud speaker)* BEAUTIFUL AFTERNOON

MARGARET is busy trying to set up the shot while PETE waves at
ERICA

Margaret   Do you know her?

Pete   No idea

PETE shouts over to ERICA

Pete   HELLO THERE. WE'RE ACTORS

Erica   ARE YOU? WHAT FUN.

Pete   I'M A PIRATE

Erica   OOOOO!

Pete   SHE'S A FEMALE PRINCESS WARRIOR

Erica   SOUNDS EXCELLENT

Pete   WE'RE ON OAK ISLAND HUNTING FOR
                                       THE ARK OF THE COVENANT

Erica   REALLY? I THOUGHT WE WERE ON
                                       BRIGHTON PIER

PETE laughs hysterically

Margaret   *(to PETE)* Camera's rolling

PETE and MARGARET get into their first positions

Margaret   ACTION

PETE doesn't move

Margaret   Pete…

Pete   I didn't hear you say action

Margaret   ACTION

Pete   Well I can't do it now. I'm not a performing monkey, Marge. Let's reset

Erica   *(through loud speaker)* ACTION

MARGARET and PETE leap into their first positions and perform

Margaret   What's going on?

Pete   There's a wedding

Margaret   Oh, is there?

Pete   Yes. And you, are not welcome

Margaret   What?

Pete   I'm letting go. You never loved me

Margaret   I cannot leave this island. My people need me

Pete   My ship needs me

Margaret   What about the treasure?

Pete   That's my treasure

Margaret   I'll fight you for it

PETE launches his first parry to MARGARET

Margaret   WRONG FOOT

MARGARET falls off the edge of the pier into the water

Erica laughs hysterically

Erica   *(through loud speaker)* WOMAN
                              OVERBOARD

PETE then panics, rips off his floral, velveteen waistcoat and goes in after her

Erica   *(through loud speaker)* MAN OVERBOARD.

PETE/MARGARET are struggling against the current

Erica   I'M COMING IN

ERICA climbs down the high chair. THE LIFEGUARD has entered hearing the commotion. ERICA shoves the loudspeaker into his hands

The Lifeguard   What's going on? Honestly, I leave you for
                              one minute and all hell breaks lose

Erica   I've got to help them

The Lifeguard   You can't help them. You don't know what
                              you're doing

Erica   I do. I told you I'm a strong swimmer. I can
                              do this. Please. Trust me. I'm not stupid

The Lifeguard watches as she bolts towards the edge

The Lifeguard   WAIT

ERICA stops

THE LIFEGUARD grabs his float

The Lifeguard   YOU'RE GONNA NEED THIS

ERICA runs back to get the float

Erica   Thank you

She plants a huge kiss on his cheek

Erica   Tell mum I love her

ERICA is off

*A huge splash as ERICA enters the water. A little business as ERICA
manages to get PETE and MARGARET to safety*

Pete   You saved our lives

PETE hugs ERICA

Pete   (to MARGARET) Oh Margey. Thank god
                              you're alive

PETE hugs MARGARET

THE LIFEGUARD throws them a rope

The Lifeguard   ERICA, GRAB THE END

They are pulled onto shore

THE LIFEGUARD helps ERICA out of the water

The Lifeguard   Are you all right?

Erica   I feel great

The Lifeguard   What you did was really silly. You put yourself in danger

Erica   Will you just shut up. I had a blast. I feel better than I've ever felt in my life. You have a great job

The Lifeguard   It was dangerous. But it was brave. And sort of silly. I'm proud of you. Shall I walk you home?

Margaret   We should get the camera

PETE helps MARGARET out of the boat. They head off towards the pier

The Lifeguard   Are you all right?

Erica   I'm fine

The Lifeguard   I should have been here

Erica   I'm sure you're mother needed you more

The Lifeguard   She broke another vase

Erica   Maybe it's time you got her that china shop

ERICA and THE LIFEGUARD kiss.

Scene 6

Brighton Pier. Wedding bells. MARGARET and PETE throw biodegradable confetti at the newlyweds, ERICA and THE LIFEGUARD. They take a seat as PETE bounds onto a makeshift stage.

Pete Mr and Mrs…. *(he forgets their surname)* Lifeguard…Margaret and I would like to perform to you, a little scene what we wrote. We hope you enjoy it. MUSIC MAESTRO

MARGARET switches on a tape recorder and plays Mozart's Clarinet Concerto in A Major

PETE goes into character as the pirate. MARGARET walks on as the female princess warrior. They walk around each other as if in a dance. They embrace and then go into the tableau of the battle scene. They perform the choreographed fight as if a choreographed dance between two lovers. PETE recites his poem during the action

Pete This year, I shall let go of hurt, This year, I shall let go of pain, I shall hold fast my sail
And let choppy seas ride me home
To shore, far, far away.
Far from guilt, and shame, and rivers deep
With ash from dead men's grief,
Fed to all regret and hatred be
Those memories, are now lost at sea. For on this shore,
I'll comfort thee
and nurture not those feelings
sad, of pain and hate and loss and strife, For life is but a wave,
And we, but merchants of the sea, Sailing on in harmony.

MARGARET and PETE reach their final tableau: 'Love's Hero'.

Applause.

Pete   And now, we dance

MARGARET and PETE dance to the music.

The sun begins to set on Brighton Pier. THE LIFEGUARD takes ERICA's hand and leads her in a dance.

ACKNOWLEDGEMENTS

Firstly, we would like to express our gratitude to all those who have been involved throughout *Found In Translation* and for making this book possible. In particular, words of gratitude go to the brilliant collaborators we met in care centres in Lewes, Brighton and London, who supplied us with weeks of enjoyment through conversation, tea and cake, fun and games and even sharing some very personal and emotional thoughts. Each and every person we met in the workshops became a friend and we thank them for allowing us into their lives. Their ideas, memories and words are at the core of this work, giving it the vibrancy and diversity that makes this book unlike any other. On this note, we would have never met our collaborators without the accommodating care centres we visited. Thank you to The Phoenix centre, Claydon House, Wayfield Avenue, Knoll House, Ireland Lodge, Craven Vale, Norton House, Darwin House and Darwin House and ETAT at The Thamesbank centre for welcoming us into their working place and being so co-operative during each step of the project. The Dot Collective cannot express enough gratitude to the fantastic team of creatives involved in the project. Writers, Alexander Moschos and Hester Kent and actors Alys Scratchley and Stuart Turner were key to running the workshops, unravelling and translating ideas into plays, bringing them alive. Their warmth and enthusiasm during the workshops generated an encouraging atmosphere meaning everyone in the room forgot their troubles and were happy! There was also Chris Levens, our superb actor who came in at the last moment with focus and professionalism for the rehearsal and performance stage. There was also the one and only (life saver) stage manager, Ariel Harrison who held the tour together to the upmost professional standard. We must not forget the lady who developed the final plays just that step further, stage director Maja Milatovic-Ovadia. Her intelligence and insight gave the plays their three dimensions, and if we had given her a longer rehearsal period, she may even have found a fourth. Thank you to the wonderful tenor, Allan Clayton who provided the most beautiful music at the drop of a hat, and for his constant support from beginning to end of the project.

Of course this project would not have been possible without the support of our many funders including Arts Council England & National Lottery, Age UK Brighton & Hove, The Dementia Action Alliance of Brighton and Hove, Lewes Town Council, The Sussex Community Foundation, The Chalk Cliff Trust, Churchill & Vincent Square councillors, Ward Budget of The City of Westminster and Spice Innovations. Without their financial support, we could have never reached 100 participants and over 250 audience members living in care. We must also mention the support in development of the project through the Dementia Action Alliance, in particular those from Lewes, Brighton & Hove and Southwark. Their guidance and information on dementia was vital to our project and carrying it out in the most beneficial way for those living with dementia and memory problems. We were privileged to receive such support in kind from arts venues and companies who had belief in the project. These include The Blue Elephant Theatre who promoted and staged the world premiere of these plays and to Longfield Hall Trust for giving us their beautiful building to perform and rehearse in. Thank you to White Light for providing us with top theatrical lighting and sound equipment so we could transform care home spaces into a theatre.

The Dot Collective would like to say thank you to all the friends, family and colleagues who have supported this charity's work from its first steps in December 2015. Their words and inputs have played a tremendous role in our decision to persevere with the work of this charity and this project. Their positive influence is instrumental to the work we have and will continue to carry out. Lastly, we must thank Dorothy May Harling, whose memory not only sits within the name of this charity but also within her teachings of values, enthusiasm and dedication to what one believes in. So, as she would say, 'take care yourself'.

ACKNOWLEDGEMENTS

The following funders have supported *Found In Translation*

FOUND IN TRANSLATION